The Leading Ladies in My Life

Poems by

Sharon Waller Knutson

In memory of Anna Lecta Madole Waller McCorkle (1881-1978), Emma Jessie Stanton Marvin (1884-1964), my beloved grandmothers, and Marvel Naomi Marvin Waller (1911-1999) my beautiful mother.

Acknowledgements

The following publications published these poems in one form or another:

Dancing With a Scorpion (Moon Journal Press 2006): "I Swear on my Mother's Grave," and "When Mama Sang."

My Grandmother Smokes Chesterfields (Flutter Press 2014): "Déjà Vu," "I Can Picture My Father's Mother," "My Grandmother's Face," "Perfect Son," "Time Travel" and "The March Wind Blows a Gale."

What the Clairvoyant Doesn't Say (Kelsay Books 2021): "Babs and Her Big Black Purse" (as "The Day After My 100-year-old Aunts Funeral") and "Staying Alive With Sharlene" (as "Numerology or Telepathy.")

Lothlorien: "Family Tree," Howdy Doody Stranger," "Rooming with Bev in Butte," Social Media Unsavvy" and "Watching the Neighbors."

Orange Room Review: "Déjà Vu" and "Perfect Son"

Red Eft Review: "Funeral Planning With Phyllis," "My Mother and Rita Hayworth" and My Mother is Not a Crier."

Silver Birch Press One Good Memory Series: "Alice in Candyland."

Storyteller Poetry Review: "Getting the Royal Treatment," "I Want Something Live, I tell Santa," "My Mother is a Marvel" and "Taking Care of Emma."

The Beatnik Cowboy: "Rounding Up Cowboys With Julia" (as "Wild Wild West.")

Verse Virtual: "Babs and her Big Bad Purse"" (as "The Day After My 100-year-old Aunt's Funeral,") "Burping Babies With Linda and Sue," "Going Crazy With Betty" and "Smoking With Copaline."

Your Daily Poem: "Christmas Chocolate Cherries," "Daddy's Three Girls" and "Sisterly Love."

Contents

PROLOGUE

Family Tree

I like to think I am a Mcintosh
surviving the frost, ripe
and red, ripped from a branch
in the March wind in Montana
with a tough skin and tender
flesh like the many apples
before me. Or a prickly pine
cone dropping to the bare
ground from the tall tree,
keeping my seeds safe
from the cold and predators,
releasing them in a sizzling summer
to procreate and protect.
Or a green leaf from a strong oak
drifting like a dragonfly,
swift and agile as my ancestors.

Social Media Unsavvy

I sign up for Facebook
to communicate with grandkids
when they don't answer
phones, emails or texts
because they are too busy
posting photos, emojis,
slogans and expressing

emotions to virtual
friends who speak the same
language. I find myself
in a foreign country feeling
like a spy or a stalker
and wish we could go back
to the days when I exchanged
long letters with my grandmothers.

I got a chance to show off
my perfect penmanship,
on stationery with flowers
or animals, lick a stamp
and envelope seal
and mail it at the post office.

I would check our mail
box every day after school
for a perfumed penned letter
from Montana or Idaho
signed XXX 000 Grandma.

I didn't even need to look
at the envelope to tell
which Grandma was writing,
The teacher wrote in cursive
and the high school dropout
who got married as a teen
printed in block letters.

.

Howdy Doody Stranger

My six-year-old great grandson
climbs in the car of a stranger
who takes him to school
and then he tells his teacher,

Stranger didn't steal me. Proof
that all the warnings: *Don't
speak to or go with a stranger*
drilled in his head as often

as the flashing lights
in the school crosswalk
are blocked out like a blast
from a boom box.

In the forties, when I am six
I accept rides with strangers
who pull to the side of the street
because refusing would be rude

and foolish since the walk
to school is long and cold
and windy and my family
applaud me for being smart

and social and safe on streets
where strangers never snatch
children with Buffalo Bob
and Howdy Doody in charge.

PATERNAL GRANDMOTHER

Getting the Royal Treatment

My grandmother is named
Anna after Anne Boleyn
and Tolstoy's Anna Karina
which may explain why
she expects royal treatment.

When I ride the Greyhound
from Montana to Idaho to visit
my grandmother, the first thing
I see when the bus pulls
into the station is the blue bird
perched on my grandmother's hat.

She squints in the sun, wearing
a colorful dress to match
her hat and sensible shoes.
We walk down the sidewalk
to the shoe store where she plops
down in a chair and summons
the clerk with a flick of her wrist
to bring her box after box of shoes
which she rejects as too big,
too small or unattractive.

The clean-shaven young clerk
obeys her command but behind
her back points to the bird on her hat
and covers his mouth to suppress
snickers, which she never hears,

but I do. I with ears sharp
enough to hear birds chirping outside
despite the canned pop music blasting
inside the air-conditioned store.

Even though he makes fun
of my grandmother, I buy
a pair of tennis shoes
because I know Anna
is not in the store to buy shoes.
Her closet is too crowded.
She is there to be waited on
and treated like the Queen
she believes herself to be.

I Can Picture My Father's Mother

Slapping knuckles with her ruler
as she stands in front of the blackboard,
eye glasses perched on her nose,
dark waist long hair coiled in a bun.

Knocking on doors to collect debts
run up by desperate housewives
who charged bread and milk
at my grandfather's corner grocery store.

But I can't picture her handing over
her life savings to a handsome gigolo
who leaves her waiting at city hall
while he flees the country with her cash

.

until I read the headline
Conman Bilks Lonely Widow
and see my grandmother's name
printed in black and white.

My Grandmother's Rules for Summer Vacation

*No playing until after your work
is done.* While my friends
play outside, I am on my knees
mopping and my grandmother
is pointing out the spots I missed.

*You must wear a hairnet
to bed. I don't want hair
all over my pillowcase.*
Does she think I am
a stray cat that sheds?

No shorts, she says
as I unpack my suitcase.
*I won't have sweaty
legs on my sofa.* I sweat
in slacks and long dresses.

*No eating between
meals,* she says
at lunchtime when I
ask to save my pie
for a mid-afternoon snack.

No pouting, she says
when holding back tears
I tell her my mother

always fixes me a snack
in the afternoon. At 3 pm

my grandfather says
he is taking me to Baskin
and Robbins. *Can I come?*
my grandmother asks
and pouts when he says *No*.

Perfect Son

The summer I turn eight
my grandmother tells me
how she dressed my father
and his sister like dolls,
how still they sat balancing
tea cups on their knees
at her ladies auxiliary parties.

She shows me his report cards,
A's lined up like Christmas trees,
the drawer filled with Boy Scout badges,
his teachers certificate in a silver frame,
next to a picture of my father in cap and gown
his dark eyes shining with promise.

She never talks about the days
she sat on the porch step,
empty cash box in her hand,
waiting for his return, while
my father swigging whiskey,
toured the country
in the back of a box car.

She never mentions the nights
she eagerly jumped out of bed
to take his collect calls, just to hear
his voice, the hours she spent
drawing the thousands of dollars

from her account, wiring the money
for bus tickets never purchased.

My father surprises us with a visit,
face flushed, grinning too much,
my grandmother giddily hugs him,
bustles off to make tea, leaving me
standing stiffly, smelling his whiskey
breath as he folds me in his arms.

Sick Bed

I've taken to my sick bed. I think
It's my time. Could you come visit?
my grandmother writes from Idaho.
I have vacation time coming so I
write back that I will take the train
from Butte to Idaho Falls and she
sends me her apartment key.

When I walk up the sidewalk,
I notice no newspaper on the step,
the mailbox is empty and I swear
I glimpse her face in the window
but when I reach her bedroom,
her white head lies on the pillow,
her body is covered in blankets,
and her eyes are closed.

As soon as I turn to go to the spare
room, I hear a weak rasp and see
spotted hands reaching for her glasses
on the bedside. When she sees me
she says in a weak voice: *Bring me*
my bottles of pills and a glass of water
from the spring water spigot
and for dinner I want a cup
of chamomile and clear broth.

She never gets out of her nightgown
or the bed except when I help

her to the bathroom where she gives
me instructions on where to find
the Dove soap and wash cloths
and towels for her bed baths. Neither
the doorbell or phone ever ring
so I jump at the strange sound on Saturday.

I heard you were in town, says my college
roommate. *Mother and I are going
to the latest Aladdin movie and we hoped
you and your grandma would join us.*
I whisper into the phone so not to wake her.
*I would love to but I can't leave Grandma.
She is too sick to get out of bed.*

What's wrong with her? she asks.
Weak heart, I say because every time
I suggest taking her to the doctor
or going grocery shopping, she'd clutch
her heart and groan, *It would kill me
to leave the house.* I look up and Grandma
is standing in the doorway, her long white
hair covering her nightgown. In a loud
voice, she asks, *Who is on the phone?*

When I tell her who and what they want,
her dark eyes sparkle and she says, *Tell them
we'd love to go and ask what time they will
pick us up.* She practically skips to the shower
instead of leaning on me as I lead the way.
I hand her the shampoo and soap made
especially for her scalp and skin that she
orders in the catalogue and is shipped to her door.

As flowers bloom on her dress and hat,
she laughs and smiles all through the movie
and in the coffee shop next door where she
eats apple pie ala mode like a starving stray
she discusses the movie in detail. I am amazed
at how strong her body and voice are and how
her pale face is glowing under the florescent
light. She blushes when the young male waiter
calls us all young ladies and kisses her hand.
.

As I pack my bag to leave, she clutches her heart
and crawls under the covers. But when I mention
a nursing home, she insists she'll be fine.
As I ride away in the taxi, I watch her in the window
standing on sturdy legs, hair wound in a bun,
waving and smiling, healthy and happy
that her granddaughter had waited on her
hand and foot and kept her lips zipped.
Neither of us expected when I left
that day that she would live to be ninety-seven.

Déjà Vu

As soon as the La-Z-Boy
delivery men leave,
my husband,
in oil stained pants,
ball point pen protruding

from his shirt pocket,
Pepsi can in hand,
walks toward the recliner,
blooming like a red rose
on the green carpet.

Before he can plop down,
I whip out the rainbow
colored crocheted blanket
my mother draped over
her easy chair to cover
the cat claw marks.

Flash back to a memory
of my grandfather
napping on the couch
my grandmother has kept
wrapped in plastic for forty years,

and me at ten repeating over and over,
I will never be like her.

MATERNAL GRANDMOTHER

Taking Care of Emma

Emma means whole or universal
which may explain
why my maternal grandmother
is my everything.

She is a heroine to me
even before I learn
of Emma of Normandy,
and Jane Austin's Emma,

which is why I always stop
at her house on my way home
from school.to check on her
after Grandpa dies and she is alone.

One afternoon, I take a different
route where I pick up bread
at the bakery and milk and eggs
at the downtown grocery store.

As I reach for my pajamas,
I sense my grandmother
is in danger and needs me.
Go to bed, my father says

and yells: *You are grounded*,
as I grab my coat and rush
out into the cold winter air
and run to the end of the block.

There I see flashing lights
on an ambulance parked
in front of my grandmother's
house and race to her rescue.

Broken hip, the x-rays show.
Nursing Home, the doctor says.
My grandmother shivers and shakes.
I'll take care of her, I volunteer.

I pack my bags and move in,
and after I poach her eggs
and make her coffee, mother
shows up and I go to school.
When Grandma is walking,
we take care of each other
until my father insists
I move back home.

We hug and hold back tears.
 I don't want to go, I say.
Your father is the boss, she says.
I want you to stay but I'll be fine.

Fast Forward to the Future,

When I work at the Billings-Gazette
I drive to Columbus in my 1955 Ford
Thunderbird. She scrambles down the steps
and opens the car door as I skid to a stop.

One weekend, I call and say I can't come
on Sunday and she is silent. *Are you okay?*
I ask. *No,* she answers in a hoarse voice.
What's wrong? I ask. *I don't know*, she says.

Grandma's sick, I tell my Aunt Copaline
Mom is never sick, she says. *I'm driving
there right now*, I respond. *Stop by
and pick me up,* she says and hangs up.

When we walk up to the porch,
the front door is wide open
and through the screen, we smell
fried chicken, biscuits and peach cobbler.

Grandma stands in her best slacks
and sweater at the stove stirring
gravy in a frying pan, her face
flushed from the steam.

Mash the potatoes and set the table,
she says in the same strong voice as she did
when Copaline was seventeen and I was two.
We stare at each other, then burst out laughing.

Mom, let me help you. You're sick,
Copaline says snatching the spoon.
Don't be silly. Glad my favorite
girls could stop by for supper.

My Grandmother Smokes Chesterfields

tosses the glowing butts on the sidewalk
and stomps them out with her boots
as she walks to the store every night

in her brown slacks to buy a six pack
of Schlitz. She pulls out her church key
and curses as beer spurts from the can.

The clerk stares at her nicotine
stained fingers and she ignores
the whispers and snickers

Women Do Not Do That
from ladies in full skirts
and manicured nails who drink

wine out of glasses and smoke
behind lace curtains
in the tiny town in Montana.

She feels she has earned the right
to smoke, drink, cuss and wear slacks
in public when she turns sixty-five

since she did what was expected of her:
married her childhood sweetheart,
birthed ten children, buried one of them

and her husband. The nine who live
have scattered like the feed
she throws out to the chickens.

The March Wind Blows a Gale

My father is off to war
and mother washes dishes

when I show up early
with a full head of dark hair,
long spider legs and skin

the color of lemon peel.
There are no incubators
in the early forties

so the doctor sends me home
with my mother and grandparents
to shrivel up and die.

But my grandmother
will have none of it.
She gets out the heating pad

and wraps it around
my blanket and I sleep
in a warm cocoon.

My only baby picture
taken two months later
shows a plump infant

with a goofy grin
and skin the color
of strawberries and cream.

Pendleton Jacket

When I am sixteen, my grandmother
receives a Pendleton jacket for Christmas
from my aunt, the police chief's wife,
and says she'll *save it for nice.*

The checkerboard red and black
beauty was on my Christmas list.
But it was a luxury my father could not afford
on his teacher's salary. I turn green as grass

as she hangs the jacket in the closet
never to be worn, like the blouses and slacks
she gets for Christmas every year. *Nice*
never comes since my grandfather died.

Every morning when I stop by before school,
I sneak into the closet and feel the tartan wool
warm on my skin as I slip the jacket off the hanger
and onto my shoulders where it fits perfectly,

feeling prettier, smarter and more popular
as I inhale the new factory fragrance.
One morning I see her reflection in the mirror.
You look nice. You'll be late. Scoot, she says.

I wear the Pendleton to school every day, returning
It to her closet in the afternoons, in case my aunt
visits. Then my father announces we are moving
at the end of the summer to another state.

In August, when I say goodbye to my grandmother,
the jacket is gone. *I put it away for nice,* she says.
When I unpack my suitcase, I find the Pendleton
nice and comfortable with my sweaters and skirts.

Even though I am her age now and she has been gone
for decades, I still hear her whispering in my ear,
Save it for Nice and I obey as I hang up my new jeans
and wear the faded ones with the tear in the knee.

My Grandmother's Face

is wrinkled as a Shar Pei
as she lies on the smooth
white sheets, eyes closed

in the same hospital
where I was born
twenty-five years before.

She is in a coma
and can't hear you,
my aunts tell me

but I pick up her limp
hand and talk to her
like I always did.

When I say goodbye,
her bony fingers grasp
my wrist like handcuffs

and she won't let go
until I say I will stay.
Then her fingers relax

and she leaves me
sitting there holding her hand
before I can leave her again.

MOTHER

My Mother is a Marvel

I never knew anyone named Marvel
except my mother and whenever
I mention Marvel Naomi Marvin
was my mother's birth name,
I am besieged with giggles
so I imagine even in the early 1900s
she was bullied and teased.

My mother is truly a Marvel.
meaning *to wonder and admire,*
as she rises in the morning
before my sister, father and me, slips
into the bathroom to apply liquid
makeup, lipstick and mascara

and long after we are in bed
and after my father falls to sleep,
she sneaks back into the bathroom
and smooths Ponds Cold Cream
all over her face and with cotton
balls erases all trace of color.
I never use soap on my face, she says.

Makeup applied to perfection,
hair ratted and secured by a scarf,
in her early eighties but looking sixty,
she sits in the passenger seat
of the bronze Lincoln as I drive
her to the specialist in Salt Lake City

after she says she can't make out
shapes of faces. *Macular Degeneration,*

he diagnoses. She never winces
or complains of pain on the six-hour drive
but the next day she stops at the top
of the stairs carrying the clothes basket
*I want to hang the sheets on the line
but my back hurts too bad,* she says.

The general practitioner takes x-rays
and sends her home. She is still
wearing her makeup and dress
from the doctor's visit when I find
her lying on her back on the sofa.
I can't get up. The pain is unbearable,
she says. *Every bone in her back is broken
from the bone cancer, the doctor* says.

Should I call an ambulance? I ask
and he answers *yes.* But when we get
to the hospital, the administrator says:
No beds. Take her home. I bite my lip
to keep from screaming, while my mother,
the Marvel that she is, lies calm and quiet
on the gurncy. A paramedic squeezes
my hand and whispers, *I'll handle this.*

He turns to the administrator and says:
May I have a word? and they disappear
behind closed doors. The door opens
and my mother is given the bed

of a patient who is in surgery. *What
if he is too weak to go home?* she frets.

I never see my mother without makeup
until I walk into her hospital room
where she lies, hiding her naked face
and the oncologist hoping for healing
but not promising handing her chemo pills.
She refuses the I-V chemo to protect
the loss of her thick head of hair.

I don't recognize the old woman
with the oatmeal mush complexion,
naked pale lips and no eyebrows.
shrinking in the sheets.
She gestures towards her purse.
*Help me put on my makeup.
My baby brother is coming to visit.*

The bones heal and with the help
of a walker, she gets along fine
for a few years until the cancer
returns and repeated chemo
weakens her heart and she falls
in the closet searching for her cat
and breaks her leg, After the surgery,
she is confused and doesn't know
where she is and why her nurse's
aide is missing. *Terri is back,* she chirps
the last day we speak.

She is going to spend the night
and shampoo and curl my hair.

She dies that night just hours
before the doctor arrives to
deliver the news that the cancer
is in remission again and write
the order to transfer
her to a nursing home.

When Mama Sang

Mama never sang on Broadway
nor at the Metropolitan Opera.
She only sang in the kitchen

as she tossed the salad,
mashed the potatoes,
fried the chicken in the skillet.

And when she hit the high notes,
the wine glasses would play flute music
and the pan lids crash like cymbals.

The dog and cat would sing backup,
one tenor and the other alto,
 their tails drumming against the wall,

while I waltzed with the broom
and my sister tap danced
on the hardwood floor.

My Mother and Rita Hayworth

My mother curls and dyes
her hair henna red, paints
her lips and cheeks Revlon rose,
and wears high heels, hose and skirts
like Rita Hayworth, imagines

romancing Cagney and dancing
with Astaire, Kelly and Sinatra
as fans flock to see her on the screen,
posing in negligees for pinup calendars
and wedding a prince on the Riviera,

as she marries my father in front
of a justice of the peace, fries us
bacon and eggs, brown bags PB&J
sandwiches with an apple and we praise
her fried chicken and mashed potatoes.

Even as Hayworth's fame and memories
fade, my mother still curls and dyes
her hair red and wears makeup, skirts,
hose and high heels to hang the wash
on the line and vacuum the rugs.

My Mother is Not a Crier

and neither am I so I am not surprised
she is not sobbing when she calls me
and says, *I tried to wake your father
but he was cold and blue. The paramedics
are on their way. Please hurry.*

I drive clear across town, expecting to see
my father sitting in his recliner drinking
a cup of hot coffee and I prepare to hand him
his carton of Camels and box of chocolates
he told me to buy him the night before.

We stand frozen as two men wheel a black bag
out of the bedroom. *Do you want an autopsy?*
a policeman asks my mother. We both stare
speechless. We are two marooned sailors
lost at sea. *He thinks we killed daddy*, I whisper.

I'm off shift, he says, *I'll be happy to stay.*
But we smile and say we are fine. When I return
the cigarettes and candy unopened, the clerk
is confused. *My father is dead.* My voice cracks
like thin ice on a deep lake where I am skating.

Time Travel

My eighty-six-year-old mother
calls me in the evening
to remind me to pick up flowers
for my father's grave
and a birthday card for my sister.

When I return at midnight,
summoned by a neighbor
who has found her wandering
the streets in her nightgown,
she has forgotten we ever existed.

It is like she has been transported
in a time machine back to the thirties
when she lived on a Montana farm
with her parents and four sisters
and three brothers, all gone now.

We sit in the emergency room
waiting for the time machine
to return her back to the nineties
and us and just as the doctor
admits her, she is back.

She wants to know what she is doing
in the hospital and why in the heck
we are asking her such stupid questions
and why am I not at Wal-Mart picking up
the flowers and the birthday card.

My Mother's First Name

is not known to many
because she puts Mrs.
in front of my father's initials.

Only his name
appears on the mailbox,
in the telephone book
and on all the bills.

When he dies, my mother
refuses to remove his name
from the phone book
or the mailbox and add hers

and gets upset when his name
disappears on envelopes addressed
by friends and relatives. I choose
 to keep his name, she says.

When strangers ask for him,
she tells them he is not home
as if he has just gone to the store
for bread, milk and cigarettes.

She refuses to leave the home
they share for fifty years
as if she fears he could not find her
when he decides to come home.

I Swear on my Mother's Grave

I am nothing like her. She
would be in the kitchen
up to her elbows in suds,

her hair curling in the steam
as the potatoes, meat, and vegetables
simmered in perfect harmony.

Or she might be out in the yard
on her knees yanking weeds
from the flower garden.

Or reaching on her tip toes,
clothespins in her teeth,
to capture the galloping sheets.

She never would be sitting
on her derriere staring
at a blank computer screen

or thumbing through a thesaurus
as she reached for words
flitting through her mind like fireflies

escaping the jar, the school of fish
racing past the dangling worm and
falling stars that melt before reaching earth

while the chicken was being cremated,
the potatoes sat on the counter in brown suits
instead of naked in the boiling water

and the broccoli crowns huddled in the fridge.
As the smoke detector shrieks
mother would be dashing through

the rooms, opening windows snatching
the skillet from the burner with oven mitts
and defrosting another chicken, but since

she isn't here, she peers over my shoulder
between the big and little dipper and watches
as the words fall into their places on the screen.

Watching the Neighbors

I used to say when I grew old
I would never be like my mother
and stand at the window
with binoculars and give

a play-by-play account
of what the neighbors
are doing, but here I am
running to the kitchen

window and watching
the Palomino and Appaloosa
eating hay, tails swatting flies,
the black and white cow

patiently nursing her calf,
still wet and wobbly,
as the crows caw
and the white tail deer

dance like ballerinas
waiting for their turn
to get a swig of water
and repeating every detail

to my husband
as he sips coffee
and birdsong plays
in the background.

SISTER

I Want Something Live I Tell Santa

It is Christmas 1944
when I am almost three.
I open a box and find a lifeless doll
instead of a live baby brother
or sister that my parents
had been promising me for seven months.

I throw the doll on the floor and pout.
Why couldn't you put what's in your tummy
in the box so I'd have something live
to play with? I ask. *We could put it back.*
Mama and Daddy just laugh.

Feb. 24, 1945
I have to admit, when they place
the scarlet faced squalling baby
in my lap, I wish I had a puppy
instead, because he would lick
my face but when my baby sister
looks up at me with her big
brown eyes and stares at me
like I am her everything, I become
her smitten slave and although
sometimes she stinks and vomits
up white stuff on my clean clothes,
I still don't want to put her back
where she came from.

Although she doesn't attend church,
our mother always sends us to Sunday
School and Bible School in the summer.
Maybe that is why she named
my sister Judith, meaning
 "Woman of Judea" in Hebrew.

Judy, as we call her, bawls
all the time and I am blamed.
What did you do to make her cry?
 my father shouts. She bawls louder.
She cries because she is a bawl
baby, I say and he sighs.
Just be nice to your baby sister.

Slow Wins the Race

My grandfather tells me when I race
around the yard like a mad hare.
But I suppose he could be talking
about my baby sister, the tortoise.

Mother said I was talking at six months,
even saying big words, but Judy is mute
for what seems like forever.
*That's because you always answer
for her,* my father says.

When she does talk, she can't say
my name so she calls me Share-nee
and soon my cousins call me that.
Pay no mind, my mother says.
*You are named after The Rose
of Sharon,* a symbol of beauty.
But I feel ugly as everyone calls
my baby sister beautiful.

*I'm not taking Judy to the store
anymore,* I complain, *She eats
all the grapes,* But she is so cute,
blonde curls corkscrewing
around her baby face, which sits
squarely on her shoulders
like play dough that my father
and even the clerk ignore her
not having a neck and stealing

grapes even though I get scolded
for not watching my baby sister.

She's the Me Too Kid, my father
explains but it is still annoying
when I recite ABCDEFG
and like a puppet she repeats
them after me, even when
I get them wrong. She bawls
when she can't go to school
with me, even though I let
her chew on my crayons.
When I practice for plays
she memorizes my lines
and learn them before me.

To get even when we visit
Grandma in Idaho and she takes us
to the hotel café to sip nasty
tasting tea and eat rice with chop
sticks, I say mean things
to my sister if my grandmother
and her friend everybody calls
Jap Mary pay more attention
to her than me which they always do.

When we are alone sliding
down the banisters, I say:
*You're adopted. Jap Mary
is your mother,* and laugh
when she bawls and screws
up her face and her dark eyes
get all squinty and slanty.
Now they'd call that child abuse,
fat shaming and racist
but that was the forties.

Montana is a Dangerous Place

my husband says as he turns
off the TV after we watch
bodies being bloodied
and bludgeoned in the state
where we were born and bred
by bad guys masquerading
as good guys and gals
on *Big Sky* and *Yellowstone*.

I think of my sister and I
hiking the Absaroka-Beartooth
Mountains, fly fishing and floating
on the Stillwater River,
and riding our Shetland pony
with Daddy on Zephr,
his white Appaloosa
as Pepper our fox terrier
and Red Boy, the collie
we boarded run beside.

In the westerns we watch
for 20 cents at the theatre
in the fifties, the Lone Ranger
and Tonto and Roy Rogers
and Gene Autry shoot the outlaws.

Murder is only make believe
in the movies and death not real
until our maternal grandfather

dies in his seventies of natural
causes and although life was never
the same we've always felt safe
in Montana's Big Sky country.

Wolf at the Door

Mama presses the steam iron
to the Brownie Uniform
I once wore that now
belongs to my sister and then
to the green Girl Scout unform
I proudly wear. While she puts away
the ironing board, I fry the ground
beef in the skillet and pour tomatoes
and pinto beans in a pot. *I'm making*
Wolf at the Door for supper to practice
for the scout weekend campout,
I tell Daddy as he carries in
the big box of Girl Scout cookies
Judy and I will be selling door to door.
Daddy peels and dices an onion
and tosses it in the sizzling skillet
sprinkled with salt and pepper.
Judy takes out the graham crackers
and covers them with marshmallows
and chocolate and melts them
on the broiler. Daddy and Mama
always managed to keep our bellies
full and the hungry howling wolf
at the door out of our house.

It's the Waller Sisters All Grown Up

the balding friend of my father says
as my sister and I cruise around Columbus -
the hometown we left when I was sixteen
and she was thirteen - on our days off
from the Billings Gazette where I am
a cub reporter and she is the switchboard
operator. Judy, a buxom brunette,
me a slender blonde. *Baby sister?*
the reporter laughs as Judy towers
over me in her high heels.

Sharon and Judy are here,
the Yakima Herald-Republic city
editor tells his wife on the phone
as we waltz and jitterbug
with the reporters and editors
on Friday and Saturday
at the local pub, after I file
my news stories and my sister
finishes her homework
at Yakima Valley College.

That's your sister? the San
Francisco Chronicle reporter
asks me as we swing across
the dance floor and she sits
sadly on the sidelines. *Broken
Heart? I know just the guy for her,*
he says as he calls his roommate.

Obnoxious, she whispers as she
and her blind date swish past us.
But soon she is laughing with
and moving in and marrying
the man she now calls her soulmate.

Are you twins? The waitress
asks in San Diego, studying
our faces like a road map. *Sisters,*
Judy says as we eat sandwiches
and sundaes. By that time
my hair has grown out to it's
natural chestnut color and we both
have bangs and curls like the Shetland
Pony we both rode as girls.

My sister drops off my toddler
nephew and he doesn't cry
when she leaves. All day he
laughs and smiles. I am puzzled
why he doesn't miss his mommy
until she returns and his head
swivels back and forth staring
at her and me and then he begins
to sob and cling to his mother
and glare at me – the baby snatcher.

The teacher, mothers and kindergartners
all stare in disbelief when I walk
into his classroom. *Justin's Mommy,*
you look different, a little girl
with Shirley Temple curls, says.

How are you related to Jessica?
the bridesmaids at my niece's
wedding rehearsal ask me. *Aunt,*
I reply to the girls just like the man
who walks up to me at the wedding
dinner and asks, *Are you Jessica's
sister? You look just like her,* while
my niece and I both with long silky
straight blonde hair streaming
to our shoulders and slender bodies
eat at different tables and her mother,
my baby sister, sits beside me smiling
in her brunette Dutch Boy bob.

Sisterly Love

Los Angeles 1970.
It has been raining steady
for four days, cars float
in freeway rivers, houses
squat in lake like lawns.

While watching the news
in Montana my father
dials my number. No answer.
Phones my sister in San Francisco.
Heard from Sharon?

Candlestick Park 1989
The Giants and Athletics
are ready to bat it out
in the World Series
when the earth shakes.

My father sees it all
from his recliner. Dials
my sister. Gets silence.
Then calls me.
Heard from Judy?

Bitterroot Valley 2000
Daddy is long gone.
On TV from Arizona,
we watch the flames flare,
Smoke billows. *Residents*

are evacuated, the newscaster says.
You heard from Judy? my husband asks.

Tonto National Forest 2021
Flames head over the hill
straight for our property.
We are evacuated and camped
out in the rec hall. My sister
calls from Arkansas. *You Okay?*

Daddy's Three Girls

Mama in a beehive,
hose and pumps
my sister and I
in dandelion gone
to seed frizzes
and bare feet
stand on the green
grass in our identical
mother daughter
dresses mama orders
from the JC Penney
Catalogue with the money
she earns taking in washing.

In sky blue rayon with red
cherry pattern, square neck,
skirt flaring past our knees,
we all smile at daddy
in the summer sunlight
as he snaps the shutter
in the Kodak camera
in the nineteen fifties.

Now senior citizens,
my sister and I stare
at the photo in the album
still tasting mama's supper –
the creamed peas, potatoes
and strawberries we pick
in the garden and the sirloin
from Mike's Meat Market.

.My Baby Sister at Her First Zoom Poetry Reading

Her hair is gray and skin smooth as the boulders
weathered by wind, sun and rain in Montana,
California, Arkansas and Oregon. Her mother
moon face is radiant and round as she greets
friendly faces popping up on the screen.

She reads each poem from her fourth
book with the same poise and dignity
as in her thirties and forties she convinces
crowds in San Francisco to rescue strays
and give money to homeless shelters.

Her voice is as strong as her legs
climbing steep slopes from seventeen
to seventy-seven as she describes
our mother *dressed to the nines*
and father and his *hard luck cases.*

From Arizona, I lie in bed and watch
on the big screen TV as her voice jumps fences
like the fox in Arkansas and soars to the sky
like the white pelicans of Oregon and says
Zee like her toddler grandson she writes about.

As her thirty something son adjusts the sound,
I am transported back to Idaho and Washington
watching her tap dancing in her teens and twenties
across the auditorium stage in beauty
pageants as the applause swells like my chest.

Christmas Chocolate Cherries

When I was six and my sister three
my grandmother gave us each
a quarter and took us to the five
and dime to buy presents
for our parents for Christmas.

Mama loved jewelry so Judy
and Grandma were looking
through the bracelets, earrings
and necklaces. *Go get your daddy
some Old Spice*, Grandma told me.

I found a red box with a photo
of a cherry and crème filling
flowing out of a chocolate.
Queen Anne Cordial Cherries.
my grandmother read.

I had no idea what it meant
but my grandmother asked
if that was what I wanted
to get my father and I nodded
and plunked down my quarter.

My grandmother stuck it in a drawer
and said she'd help us wrap
the presents Christmas Eve.
But curious as the Calico,
my sister and I opened the box.

We held a chocolate cup
in our palms and used both
thumbs to pry them open
and with our tongues scooped
and swallowed the syrup.

Then we chewed the cherry
and the chocolate, savoring
the sweet taste and put the box
back in the drawer, repeating
the ritual night after night
until there was only one left.

Grandma gave us the wrapping
paper and we wrote *For Daddy*
on a tag and placed it under
the tree. When daddy opened
it, his dark eyes widened.
He laughed. and we giggled.

Every Christmas, it became
a game and we'd buy daddy
a box of Queen Anne Cordials
and eat all but one and he'd
feign surprise and us innocence.

The family tradition continued
even after we left home. We'd
return with jewelry and perfume
for mother and sweaters
and Queen Anne's for daddy
and eat all the chocolates but one.

This December, I ask my husband
for a box of Queen Anne's. *What
about the diabetes?* he asks. *I promise
I'll eat only one,* I lie. On Christmas
Day, I open the box and eat
the only chocolate left. My husband
laughs and I feign innocence.

MOTHER-IN-LAW

Funeral Planning With Phyllis

The way she crosses
out certain survivors
and puts them under
who *preceded her in death*
in her obituary,

and replaces names of dead
eulogy and prayer reciters
and hymn organ players
with the living in the program
she types on her Underwood,

we figure she started planning
every detail of her funeral
after she almost bled to death
in her late sixties from surgery
of a gallbladder that gave her grief.

When she dies at ninety-eight
despite insisting she would make
it to a hundred and three
we follow her instructions
with the exception of two.

I don't want a speaker. They talk
too long and might say something
bad about me, she says. Her best friend
speaks short and sweet and imagines
my mother-in-law smiling.

I don't want a public viewing.
No one wants to look at an old
lady with wrinkles, she says.
People pack the church to see
what almost a century looks like.

AUNTS

Zig Zagging with Zelma

Zelma and your father won ballroom
competitions all over the state,
Grandma Anna says as she shows
me trophies and photographs
of a slender brunette, her dark
eyes staring up at her handsome
curly haired brother as he whisks
her across the floor, and she twirls
like a Ferris Wheel, short skirt
flaring to show off shapely legs.

She graduated from teacher's college
and taught with your father, grandfather
and me in the one-room schoolhouse
in Shelley until Jim came along and took
her away from me, my grandmother says.

But she smiles as she shows me photos
of her oldest grandchild and only
grandson, Zelma's son who is a dead ringer
for my father at that age. Blair shows
off perfect white teeth and healthy gums
in his class photos. She only has one photo
of his younger sister, my cousin Ann,
who is named after my grandmother
and she is missing her front teeth.

When I am eleven, my grandmother
and I travel by train from Idaho Falls

to Kansas City, Kansas, to watch Blair
graduate from high school. When Zelma
meets us at the train, I don't recognize
this woman with the white streak
in her hair and round face.

Her voice is like velvet, her smile
shining as bright as the sun and her hug
warm as a wool blanket. Cousin Blair,
six feet tall and wiry like my father
squirms as Grandma smothers him
with attention and kisses ignoring
my cousin Ann, twelve at the time
dark eyes throwing darts at the target
on my back as she stands aside.
That's the only time I see Aunt Zelma.
But when my father dies, she calls
to tell me she is sorry and asks about
me, skirting any questions about herself.

When Zelma slips in the shower
in the assisted living center
at the age of ninety-two
and doesn't survive the surgery
to repair a broken hip, I get
a call from Blair's wife. *Sweet,*
stoic and spry, is how Marilyn
describes her mother-in-law.
She may have lived to be
one hundred if she hadn't fallen.

Mary Magdalene Meets Dick Tracy

Grandma Emma names my mother's
oldest sister, Madeline, after Mary
Magdalene, but my grandfather
wants his first born to be a boy
so he takes her to his barbershop
and when she gets out of the chair
she looks more like Dick Tracy
than Mary Magdalene.

Everyone calls her Dick
so I never even know her real
name until I am sitting at my desk
at the Billings Gazette reading
the society page when I see
my Aunt Dick's smiling face
and the name Madelaine Scott
as president or chairman
of every organization in town.

It makes sense because Aunt
Dick is always bossing
everyone in the family around
as if we are her children
or her employees. She always
knows what is best for us
and what we should and should
not do. *She does this because
she is the oldest of nine kids,*
my mother says but that doesn't

make me feel any less resentful.
You're just like her, my baby sister
says but what does she know?

My mother has her own resentments,
*I had to drop out of school
in the eighth grade to take care
of my brothers and sisters because
mother was always pregnant
and Dick never did anything
but go to school.* But she defends
her sister when I say, *Aunt Dick
hates me.* My mother tells me,
*Aunt Dick loves you. You are
The daughter she couldn't have.*
I soften. Especially when I see how
she looks at her two sons,
and how she mourned the death
of her oldest by tuberculosis.

I forgive her criticism of my parents
because they prefer to stay home
after retirement while she and Uncle
Bill travel in an RV because when
Mother is diagnosed with Melanoma
Aunt Dick instructs me to call her collect
to give her updates. I also forgive
her when I do and her voice is sharp
as scissors until I say, *She's in remission*
and she forgives me for running up
her phone bill. She dies a few months
before my mother outliving
all but four siblings and a son.

Gabbing With Geraldine

Girls named Geraldine
have the gift of gab,
are charming and cheerful.
and party girls, says
the search engine site,
describing my mother's
younger sister as detailed
as a sketch artist.

Geraldine could always
talk herself in or out
of anything, my mother
used to say. *She could*
charm a Diamond Back
into giving him her rattle,
my father would say.

Geraldine is the friendliest
aunt, my cousins and I agree,
Always leaves her door open
and greets guests with a pot
of coffee or a beer depending
on the time of day you show up.

When my Grandpa buys the bar
on the highway, and hauls
in the one-room schoolhouse
and turns it into a dance hall.,
Aunt Geraldine and Uncle Emil

drive the 14 miles between
their house and the bar on Friday
nights, drink and dance until the bar
closes down and then sober
up on Sunday and drive home
and he is back as conductor
when the train leaves the tracks.

When my mother is hospitalized
with every bone in her back broken,
I call Aunt Geraldine. *She's lucky
You're there,* she says, *Your mother
would have just lay on the couch
and died.* When I call to tell her
Mother had fallen and broken a leg,
she and I cry together because
we both fear she would die
in the hospital and she did.

I should have gone first, she says
every time she loses a loved one.
First her husband to asthma,
her teenage grandson to a drunk driver,
her oldest daughter to alcoholism
and asthma and her youngest
daughter to emphysema, She
is the first Marvin to make it to ninety.

Smiling With Snooks

Resembling her namesake Actress
Vivien Lee, my mother's younger
sister closest to her age is lively
and lovely as the Lady of the Lake
and enchantress of Merlin.

Although her birth name is Vivian
Maude, everybody calls her Snooks,
a nickname bestowed on her by a baby
sister who couldn't say her name.

When I am born, Aunt Snooks
is living in Billings and working
at a department store where she meets
and marries my Uncle Roger.
who looks just like Rock Hudson,
and moves to Butte. Aunt Snooks
is not a big part of my life
until I get a job at the Montana-Standard.

*Of course, you'll stay with us until
you get an apartment*, she says
and introduces me to the son
of one of her friends and isn't
surprised when his mother rides
along on the date and sits between
us in the car and the movie theatre.
He's a Mama's boy like my boys.

When she calls to say Uncle Roger
passed away, she is patient
when I ask: *Are you sure?*
because we are all in shock
since he is fit and healthy.
We didn't know he was struck
by a car in a crosswalk
while riding his bicycle
in downtown traffic at dawn.

We were grateful he was in a coma
and we had time to say goodbye,
she says. When my father died
at seventy-three Roger said he hoped
he lived that long and he did.

He reminds me of your grandfather,
she says when she meets my husband.
When we honeymoon in Arizona
where we plan to live, she insists
we stay in her spare bedroom
and even though her bent back
is as fragile as glass from osteoporosis
she insists on accompanying us on
the trip to view the land where we plan
to build our house and live. She winces
but she smiles as a gabby neighbor
invites us for lunch and entertains
us with stories about her hunky
son who flies back and forth
in a helicopter to Hollywood
hoping to be the next Tom Cruise.

*The firemen called me again last
night and said she fell out of bed
I told her not to get up*, her daughter says.
She doesn't know me anymore, her son says.
Who are we? I ask her as we stand
by her bedside after the aide leaves
and I pack a bag and move in.

Don't be silly, Sharon, she laughs.
And then shivers. *It's cold in here.
I want to go outside where it's warm.*
She stares out the window where she
points to all the people she sees
who are not there. I wonder if she
sees my grandparents and my mother.

Finally, a nursing home has a vacancy,
her daughter says and my husband gently
picks up Snooks and carries her to the car.
Hurt, Hurt, Hurt, she murmurs.
It's okay to go, I tell her days later
as she drifts in and out of consciousness,
but she hangs on until she hears the voice
of her oldest son who flies in from Spokane
You almost made it to ninety, I say
as I kiss her cold cheek.

The mobile home park rec hall
is crowded with friends and family
as we stare at my beautiful aunt
in her high school portrait, lively
and lovely as Vivian Leigh.

Smoking Cigarettes with Copaline

*Polio burst my dreams of being a ballerina
as a child*, my Aunt Copaline says
as she lights a Lucky Strike and takes a drag
when I am twenty and living with her
in Billings until I get an apartment.

*I started smoking when I was fifteen
right after you were born,* says my mother's
baby sister. Her limbs aren't twisted
but they are as thin and fragile
as a twig on a tree as she fries bacon
and French Toast for her three sons,

blonde, blue eyed and fresh faced
like their mother and the fourth son
with dark eyes and hair and a pointed
chin like his father. When she is forty-
two, she puffs on a Newport and sips
a Scotch in the San Francisco disco
where she jitterbugs with Uncle Frank.

She swears she's going to stop smoking
when they start a new life at the fishing lodge
on the Bitterroot River. But after he dies
at fifty-nine of a heart attack, she smokes
two packs a day of Camels as she manages
the lodge to support her teenage sons.

Back in San Francisco with her second
born son and granddaughter, she smokes
Winstons and then Virginia Slims
until a policeman knocks on the door
at 3 am to say her youngest son
has been shot in the back of the head
as he counts the money at Thrifty Drug.
That's when she switches to Marlboros.

A cigarette dangles from her mouth
even as she drags an oxygen tank
but she finally quits on the ventilator.
Emphysema, the doctor writes
on her death certificate but I know
she died of a broken heart.

Crazy Over Betty

Dummy, moron, idiot, retard, the bullies
chant as my Aunt Betty pulls the mufflers
tighter over her ears to shut out the insults
and the freezing Montana temperatures.
I can't remember, she tells the teachers
in the 1930s who try and give up
and she drops out in the second grade.
I read her Betty & Veronica comic books.
That's me and you, she says laughing.

When the kids call me *skinny stick*
and a *creep* because of my body
type, I go to my grandparents'
house and teach Betty her ABCS
and to play Go Fish. I don't care
if she forgets and I have to repeat it
over and over because Betty
eighteen years older than me
doesn't care if I am fat or skinny.

As long as we are in the safety
of her bedroom, Betty smiles
and sings silly songs but outside
she fidgets and frets and accuses
me of plotting behind her back
if I talk to anyone. *Leave me alone,*
she shrieks at strangers
who she says shout and scream.
Speechless, they stop and stare.

When Grandpa drives her
to the doctor in his truck,
we put Betty in the middle
and I sit by the door to keep
her from grabbing the handle
and jumping out on the mountain
road and into the valley below.
See all those people, she says.
All I see is rocks and a river.

After Grandpa dies and we move
across the state, Grandma calls
and says Betty is in the Montana
State Home for the Insane. *She tried
to strangle me after seeing Satan.*
Later, we learn my beautiful sexy
aunt with a habit of seducing men
was spayed like her calico.

*I'm getting married and having
a baby,* Betty says on the phone
when the nurses call with an update.
*Roy Rogers and Dale Evans invited
me to dinner*, she insists even after
Roy and Dale are dead as well as
her parents and siblings. One day,
a nurse calls and says Betty died
at eighty-three, proving the doctors
wrong. *People like her die young.*

Alice in Candyland

King trumps Queen, my mother's
younger brother, Uncle Jack
says as he teaches me to play poker.
But I prefer to watch his wife,
Aunt Alice, the woman
I want to be, as she removes
her wool coat after working
all week as the city treasurer.

She kicks off her snow boots
and heads for the kitchen
and I follow. *I'm making taffy,*
divinity and chocolate fudge
for the holidays. Want to help?
she asks me. *I don't know how,*
I say. *Don't worry. I'll teach you.*

I slide on the icy sidewalk
separating our houses on Saturday.
Like a warm sweater, Alice's big body
surrounds mine as she shows me
how to stir the sugar so it doesn't
burn on the bottom of the saucepan.

As her strong hands hold mine
while we whip the egg whites to stiff
peaks, I feel the strength to stand
up to the bullies who call me *Skinny*
Stick and when we pull the taffy,

I feel the stamina to walk two miles
to school as the snow freezes into ice.

The misery of being a thirteen-year-old
feminist female in the fifties in a small town
melts like the sweet candy in my mouth
as we stand in the warm kitchen
forming a bond that can't be broken
by distance, divorce or death, something
we didn't know that snowy Saturday
when I learned to make candy with my aunt.

Babs And Her Big Bad Purse

The day after my Aunt Bab's funeral,
my cousin and I thumb through
the family photograph albums
recalling happier times. As my aunt
peers over the back of the rocker,
he barely a year old, concern
stamped all over his freckled face,
sits holding a wrinkled infant wrapped
in a pink blanket, mouth open wide
like a baby bird begging for a worm.
All I wanted to do was protect you,
he says. I was the sister he never had
and he was better than a big brother.
But the first day of school, we are kittens
facing a pit bull when the third grader
in a giant's body holds us hostage
on the sidewalk as we walk home
until my tiny aunt – outmatched in size
and stature - storms in like a tornado
and smacks the bully in the back of his head
with her purse heavy as a hammer
pounding him like a nail as he runs
down the street blubbering and bawling.
I giggle with glee, but my cousin scowls
because he knows his mother
has given the bully more ammunition
for his taunts. *Sissy Boy. Your mama
has to fight your battles for you,*
the bully shouts, but this time
he keeps his eyes peeled to make
sure my aunt is nowhere around.

Is Sylvia Still in San Clemente?

I only heard her voice once
and it left a chill in the hot air
when I called and said I was
a block from her home and asked
if I could stop and see her
and my uncle and my three
cousins and she said, *Sorry
we have plans* and hung up.

Although I lived in the Los Angeles
area within driving distance
for several years, I took
that dismissal as a sign
I was not welcome in her life.

I had never seen her in person
since my mother's baby brother
had left Montana right
after graduation for college
in California and only returned
alone twice – for the funeral
of my grandmother and my mother's
hospitalization for melanoma
before dying of the dreaded
disease himself three months later.

I recall seeing photos
of a petite pretty brunette
smiling in a wedding gown

and in a bikini blowing out candles
on many layered birthday cakes
as their three blonde babies
barefoot in bathing suits
pranced by the pool like ponies.

If Google is to be believed,
she is alive at ninety-two
and living in San Clemente.
I picture Aunt Sylvia
a shriveled version of herself.
still smiling in the sun
by an Olympic size pool.

COUSINS

Staying Alive with Sharlene

When the speeding train slams
into the 1951 Studebaker Sedan
carrying the five senior high school
girls home for lunch, twisting
and crushing it into scrap metal,
the loud crash shakes the sidewalk

where my two cousins and I bicycle
home from elementary school.
Gerry Gene's wheat colored hair
falls in his aquamarine eyes
And Larry's freckles and red hair
sparkle in the bright sunshine
as they race to see who can
reach the finish line first.

What was that? I ask as my Little Orphan
Annie hair frizzes around my round face.
None of our eleven-year-old minds
could even imagine Gerry's sister Sharlene
with the blonde bangs and pageboy,
is being cut from the wreck
all bloodied and busted.

My mother says Sharlene survives
because her number was not up yet.
She explains that my eight cousins
out of twenty die young
because their number was up.

Not because of murder,
disease or drunken drivers.
Since my mother's number was up
at eighty-seven, she isn't here to
explain Larry's first email in seven years
as I am thinking of him and Gerry Gene.

 Gerry is dead at seventy-nine, he writes,
but Sharlene is still alive at eighty-five
and the oldest surviving cousin.
I remember the secret Sharlene
whispers to me at her wedding
to the airline pilot two years
after the accident. *I'm going*
to live forever because I will
travel by air and stay off
the roads where the idiots are.

Did my brother die? she asks
from Washington the minute
 he leaves earth from Oregon.
And on the exact time and day
a year later she whispers: *Gerry*
I am on my way and she is gone.

Burping Babies with Linda and Sue

I am surprised to see my cousins
when I show up on Saturday
at my grandmother's
house to play Go Fish with Aunt
Betty since Linda and Sue
are both married ladies
with babies born a month apart.
Just like Sue and me.

Linda is sixteen and Sue
and I just turned fifteen
and they are smoking Lucky
Strikes as they play poker
with Cousin Larry, complaining
because they had to give up
Schlitz and Scotch while
nursing their babies.

They invite me to play
with them but I'm a beginner
since I am busy writing
fiction and doing homework.
I feel like a fifth wheel since I've
never even tasted the lips
of a boy, alcohol or nicotine.

Just like I feel when my cheerleader
Homecoming Queen cousins play
pool and smoke cigarettes

with football players in their basement
while I read movie magazines.
and swing in the hammock.

To escape the swirling smoke,
Betty and I go in her bedroom
but she can't remember how
to Go Fish and I wonder why
the family fell apart after Grandpa
died choking on a chicken bone.

If he was still fixing our lives
like he repaired his junk cars,
maybe Grandma and Aunt Geraldine
and Uncle Emil would be sitting
here burping their granddaughters
instead of boozing it up in Broadway Bar.

I would have played poker with my cousins,
held and burped their babies
and called them on Sundays if I knew
Linda would die in her forties
of asthma and Sue of emphysema
shortly after we reunite after forty years
and celebrate our 60th birthdays drinking
iced tea and playing Scrabble at Lake Tahoe.

Discovering Susan's Secrets

Susan is my baby cousin, I tell the hairdresser
when we are in our fifties. *She was so cute
with those fat little cheeks.* Susan hides
her red face behind the black cloak
as the hairdresser towels her wet hair
and then begins snipping and shaping.

I didn't say she was a squirmer while Robin,
her twin brother leaned into the curve
of my arm as I held them when they
were born when I was six. It was Robin
who gave females flowers and Susan
just gave us rocks. But I was surprised
when Susan tells me she is an alcoholic,
sober sixty days when we move to Apache
Junction not far from her and my aunt.

I had shared her room for two weeks
when she was a senior in high school
and I was working in Butte. Because
we had the same dark eyes, dark hair
and slim body type, at her graduation,
everyone assumed I was her older
sister back home from college.
Susan would smile and not set
them straight because ever since
she was two and stayed with us,
for a week, whenever they visited
from across the state, Susan would

cling to my mother and follow
my sister and I around like a baby duck.

When my mother was diagnosed with cancer,
Susan rented a car and drove from Arizona
to Idaho to visit her in the hospital. *Mother
needed to see her sister, just in case,*
she says. But the way she sat
on the edge of my mother's bed
holding her hand, her doe eyes full
of fright, I knew she needed to see
the aunt she thought of as a mother.
Susan didn't look like herself.
She had gained weight and her body
was bloated and burly like her brother.
When my mother died, Susan called
and asked for one of my mother's
salt and pepper shakers to remember
her by. I regret I never got around
to giving her a memento of my mother.

Now Susan was thin again, almost gaunt.
Once she talked me into going to the casino
with her, strutting in with a fistful of dollar bills,
totaling $600. *The more you bet,
the more you win,* she explains
as she feeds the slots and rolls the dice
with the same excitement as I imagine
she had downed the whiskey shots.
When we walk out of the casino,
she is broke but laughing. *Easy come.
Easy go,* she says, high on the adrenalin.

Now she fuels her fever with caffeine.
coffee or coke. She is late for Thanksgiving
and Christmas dinners saying she was held
up at the casino. *Susan always wins,*
her mother says. *Of course,* she says
and tosses dollar bills on the table
like confetti. I don't ask how much she lost
or if she was supporting her gambling
habit with her mother's many bank accounts.

With a stiff spine and lip, she stocks
grocery shelves all day, then drives
four miles to take her mother medicine
and groceries and drive her to the doctor.
We see each other at holiday dinners
and while her mother naps, I follow
her out into the sunshine as she smokes
a Lucky Strike. *I can never please her,*
 she complains. *I'm too fat or too skinny*
 or working too hard or not enough,
she says as she puffs on a Pall Mall..
.

When Susan can't get off work to drive
my aunt to the doctor, I do and when
she checks her into the nursing home,
my husband and I help, since my aunt's
bones are so brittle she can't sit or walk.
The last time I see Susan she is dressed
in black as she stiffly hugs me goodbye
after her mother's standing room only
memorial service. A year later
her husband calls to say Susan died
of cancer. *She didn't want you to worry.*

I took care of her at home.
One day I woke up and she was gone.

The name Susan means lily or lotus flower,
which symbolizes regeneration and rebirth.
Every time a lily blooms, I see Susan's
smiling face soaking in the sunshine.

Bonding With Blood

Your cousin Ann died of cancer,
her brother's wife tells me
on the telephone. *Her fiancée*
and she were both diagnosed
the same day. He was gone
in six months. She lasted three years.
Even went back to her psychiatric practice.

Our son is getting married in Seattle.
You're invited, she says, I hadn't
seen Cousin Blair or Ann since
his high school graduation.
But my Aunt Zelma had filled
my mother in on all her grandchildren.
My mother says: *Look for a blond*
clean cut guy. He's a doctor.

There is no blond clean-cut guy
who looks like a doctor when we
arrive at the venue on Puget Sound.
I ask a guy in long dark hair flowing
to his waist where I can find the groom.
But before he answers, *I'm Chris,*

I look into my father's dark eyes
and know I have found him. *I'm your*
father's cousin which would make you
my second cousin, I say. He smiles
my father's smile and hugs me.

*My mother said you'd be blond
and a doctor.* He laughs and says
in my father's voice: *That's Ann's son.*

If you're Chris's cousin. Then you're
my cousin too, a pretty twenty
something woman with my sister's
face says. *I'm Barbara.* I hear my voice
giving orders and come face to face
with another twenty something
with my dark eyes and body and I know
I have met Barbara's twin sister.
Hi Juanita, I say, *I am your cousin.*

Soon Cousin Blair, now stocky and gray,
but still handsome, and his wife show up
and we talk like we grew up next door:
The benefit of having the same blood
racing through our veins. So when seven
years later, Barbara calls to say Chris
died of a rare form of cancer, I grieve
like I have lost my own brother.

SOUL SISTERS

Rounding Up Cowboys With Julia

The way she dangles her Pall Mall
from her poppy red lips knowing
the cowboys at the coral will whip
out lighters from back pockets
faster than a firearm, then takes
a long drag as their eyes slide

from her platinum wedge
haircut, Siamese blue eyes,
to her button-down blouse
and designer jeans
showing more curves
than a country road,

nobody can tell her daddy -
a big shot lawyer in LA -
has just dropped dead
of a heart attack and her mother
has dragged her out of UCLA
summer school and driven

her and her brother to a Wyoming
dude ranch in the early sixties
where Julia, her mother and I
serve salad, steak and stout
to cowboys and dudes. The way
she wrestles with the wrangler

on the bed of his Chevy pickup
stinking of collie and Coors
no one ever suspects she is engaged
to an LA student with the scent
of Brut and marijuana. I don't
tell anybody. So I probably am

the only one who isn't surprised
when she goes back to LA
at the end of the summer
and her cowboy gets hitched
to another waitress named Julia
the next summer on top of the Tetons.

Bunking with Bev in Butte

Bev is Wanda the Woodpecker
with her red curly hair and spectacles
making me laugh when I want to cry
as I wing my way through freezing
temperatures, slick streets and deep
dangerous mines full of dynamite.

I am Belinda the Bumblebee
with golden hair and black roots
sipping nectar and making honey
as the new female reporter in town
while she nurses broken bones
and hearts in the hospital
across the road from the brownstone

where we sleep in twin beds,
take turns baking biscuits
and chicken on our gas stove
and ordering porkchop sandwiches,
cheeseburgers and peperoni pizza
on the weekends, when we drink
Singapore slings and Grasshoppers
and jitterbug with miners, businessmen
and boys home from universities.

When she marries a tall strapping
Irish catholic who works in the mines,
and buys a three-bedroom house
in Butte, I wing my way to Washington

California, Mexico and Canada
followed by her letters of nurturing a growing
family as she nurses senior citizens.
On occasional visits, we laugh, dance
and dine on prime rib and cheesecake.

Now white haired great grandmothers
married to our soulmates.
Bev is still in Butte drilling dreams
in the Ponderosa Pines
and me in Phoenix winging it
through the desert sipping sweet
nectar and buzzing among the saguaros.

Finding a Live Body With Donna

Why don't you and your sister
live with your parents until
you get married? Donna
who lives next door in Yakima asks.

What if we never get married?
I answer. She said she dropped
out of high school to get married
because she was pregnant.

I had four kids, The police found
my husband's boat, but no body.
They won't declare him dead
for seven years, she says.

I know he faked his own death
so I am looking for a live body
to nail him for child support.
She haunts his favorite hangouts.

Her job as a waitress at the local
greasy spoon doesn't pay the bills
so she got herself a sugar daddy.
He is a married prominent politician.

He called DFS and had my kids
put in foster care to have me
to himself when he wants me.
He pays my rent and utilities.

Many years later a married man
says I need him to pay my rent
and makes me the same offer
and I laugh and walk away.

Surviving in San Francisco With Loraine

Did you ever see Al Pacino in Serpico?
The real life Serpico saved my brother's
life, after he was framed for a crime
he didn't commit, Lorraine tells me
in her New Jersey accent as we sit
on a bench at Fisherman's Wharf
in San Francisco as seagulls
try to snatch our fish and chips
wrapped in a newspaper on our laps.
I remember a bearded Pacino
in a blue beanie and beard
as Frank Serpico, the immigrant's son
who knocked down the blue wall
of silence in the NYPD.

The wind tousles my Jane Fonda
shag but doesn't touch a strand
of her dark hair sleeked back
in a bun like Joan Crawford.
I envy her natural tan as the sun
burns my skin on a Saturday
as we are relaxing after a busy
week on the San Francisco
Business News after doing
the humiliating perp walk
through the Chronicle and Examiner
newsrooms where the Managing
Editors smile and the all male
news staff smirks knowing
their jobs are safe from females.

I met one of those male chauvinist
pigs at a press conference, she says.
He treated me like a cockroach.
She describes him as speaking
with a British accent and smoking
a pipe and I recognize the Chronicle
reporter I am currently dating.
Your fellow reporter is a Lesbian,
he says as we do the jitterbug
under the flashing disco lights
and I laugh and leave the dance floor.

You will survive, Loraine says, years
later when she shows up in San Diego
on a weekend after I lose the baby
and brews chamomile tea and broth.
And when I spend the next weekend
at her house in North Beach
she says: *Sleep all day if you need to.*
Your body needs the rest. And I do.

It is the last time I see her. When
I dial her number a Chinese woman
says in Mandarin: *nĐn dĬ cuò le.*
Now I can't look Loraine up on Google
or social media without a last name
or current city and I am sure
both have changed since the seventies.
I picture her in her eighties standing
on sturdy legs in the sun surrounded
by a soulmate and grandchildren
and wonder if she remembers me.

Rowing a Boat With Merrily

Merrily says she was named after
her father, a man who was cold,
hated children and beat her
with a belt which may explain
why she didn't live up to her
Welsh name which means joyous.

She looks like an Amazon, one male
reporter snickers while another guffaws
as Merrily stomps through the newsroom
blonde hair swinging across shoulders
to her small waistline. In six-inch heels,
she stands six feet two and towers
over all of us, as we shrink in our seats.
.

She removes her shoes and in stocking
feet shuffles to her locker and slips
on her flats. Then she grabs her brush
and twists her hair in a knot. *Don't listen
to them*, I say. *I think you look like a Goddess.
They are jealous.* I even buy her the book:
Celebrate Your Inner Goddess but even though
she refers to them behind their back
as male chauvinist pigs like all the feminists
who attend the meetings where we go
every Saturday she believes them instead of me.

Pseudo feminist, the male reporters
call her. I hate to admit they are right

when she insists on getting out of bed
even when she gets her period cramps
and fries eggs and grills waffles
on the weekends when I sleep over
although her husband says:
Let Sharon do it after I offer
and calls me a slave when I take
a picnic lunch to the school and eat
with my teacher boyfriend.

When she moves back to Florida,
and I visit in June and we browse
in a tourist shop, the clerk pegs me
for a Californian. *How did you know?*
 I ask and she replies. *Your tan.*
It's too hot to sunbathe in Florida.
Merrily stomps out of the shop
while I am buying a seashell necklace
hot air slapping her in the face. *Lies.*

We all tan in Florida, Merrily fumes,
folding her buttermilk white arms.
I keep my mouth shut so she won't
throw me out into the heat. But I hate
Florida. My hair is always soaking wet,
sweat flows out of my pores like a river,
I can hardly breathe in the sauna air
and sleeping is not even in the scenario.

I am relieved when her parents
take us boating until her mother
sprays me so I stink so bad
the mosquitos halo my head

waiting for the spray to wear off
so they can eat me for a snack.

While everyone else is relaxing
and enjoying the boat ride,
I huddle in the corner waiting
for the wet waves lapping
against the boat to wash off
the spray and the mosquitos
to attack. But it doesn't happen
and I bolt as soon as the boat
reaches shore and gladly board
the plane for San Diego the next day.

In my last memory of Merrily,
blonde hair billowing
like sheets in the wind, she
merrily merrily merrily rows
rows rows her boat in Mosquito Lagoon.

Kibitzing With Karen

She is pure and clear as spring
water from a Wisconsin stream
so it is no wonder that her Danish
 parents name her Karen.

Only 5 foot 2 and less than 100
pounds and shy as a sparrow
in her twenties, I in my thirties
take her under my wing

when I first spot her sitting
silently on a stool studying
photos of brides at the Times-
Advocate where I am city hall reporter.

When she moves to the news
 section, she is assigned the desk
 in front of mine and every noon
we go to lunch at the local café.

She is silent when I say:
*He didn't come home again
last night* and hands me a towel
to wipe the vomit from my mouth

during my morning sickness
that extended to all day
and sit by my side when I miscarry
after he runs off with his secretary.

Speak up. Stop being so stupid,
her first husband Steve
tells her but his best friend
Peter says, *You're sweet*

and smart and my kind of girl.
She leaves Steve and moves
in with me until the divorce
is final and she marries Peter.

When I get back from Mexico,
I stay with Karen and Peter.
I'd sell hot dogs, I confess.
but my math is bad.
.

It makes no sense to her engineer
husband. *Just count the change
backwards,* Karen advises. I take
her advice when I sell clothes.

She quits her job after her baby
is born and Peter gets an engineer
job in San Jose. I kiss the forehead
of her blonde, blue eyed daughter

and hug Karen close and she says,
*I'm only moving across the state.
We can visit often,* but we both know
this is probably the final goodbye.

*A Sharon called saying she is homeless
in San Francisco,* she phones my sister

two years later. *It wasn't her.*
She's in Idaho running a bookstore.

I often dream about the phone ringing
and I think it is Karen on the other line.
Are you in California or Wisconsin?
but all I hear is the sound of pure clear water.

Carne With Carolina

Scent spicy as salsa,
voice musky as mustard,
skin brown as baked beans,

she sneaks a sirloin steak
into my hospital room
in Guanajuato. *Carne,*

Carolina calls dancing
deliciously, hips swaying
to imaginary music, *Meat,*

I say as we share sandwiches,
she teaches me Spanish
and I tutor her in English.

She is the only staff at midnight
and the light is as yellow
as my skin, but I can see

her young face smiling in a short
skirt as she flops on the bed
and tells me she is studying

English and nursing and plans
to immigrate to America
and sit in the sand in the sun.

Night after night, she shows
her moon face in my room
sharing snacks and dreams.

I see the sadness in her eyes
when she learns of my release,
and whispers, *See You in San Diego.*

A couple of years later, I am lying
on the La Jolla beach when I hear
a familiar voice say, *Remember Me?*

and there stands Carolina in a bikini
showing me a Scripps Hospital nametag,
her brown eyes as bright as the sun.

Running With Jenny

When she is ten, she tells me, her mother
gives her the phone number of her father's
mistress in case something happens
to her. She memorizes the number
until she leaves Milwaukee and moves
to San Diego in the seventies
and becomes a secretary tangled
in her own triangle. Her boss's wife
shows up at midnight at the motel room
shouting for *the slut who is screwing*
my husband and Jenny crawls out
the window and barefoot and naked runs
in the blackness through the parking lot
and across the backyards as her neighbors
sleep and slips through her front door
and under the covers with her sleeping
husband. The next morning Jenny sips
coffee and takes shorthand as her boss
whispers, *Are you okay?* After work,
the boss's wife sitting in the bleachers
next to Jenny's husband and me
never suspects that the six-foot tall
flat chested freckle faced redhead
with her hair tucked under her ballcap,
who slams her bat against the softball
and covers the bases like a Cheeta
and slides into home plate safely,
winning the game for the company,
is the slut sleeping with her husband.

Seeking Sandy on the Search Engine

It was lust when she jumped
on the back of the motorcycle
of the Greek guy in Athens
in her twenties but love
when she married Jacob
in Pasadena, she tells me
by snail mail in the eighties.

So I doubt the search engine
that gives Sandy single status
and she and Jacob's addresses
in separate cities. But the last time
we had lunch with them
a decade ago, he was drinking
beer before church as she frowned
and folded her arms.

That is Sandy's straight white teeth,
and apple cheekbones on the Net
Worth website for producers,
directors, writers and actors,
and probably what she looks like
today in her sensational sixties,
but I doubt if she is worth $19 million
since her claim to fame was a non
speaking part in a Jim Carey movie
and casting Shaq O'Neal's co-star
as the leading lady in one of her plays.

Another website lists her mother
at 92 and still living in the family home
where we watched from the patio
in Pasadena as green parrots
flocked to the trees to feast on
black walnuts. That was before
her father died of cancer
and her mother got Alzheimer's
and Sandy gave up her career
to be a full-time caregiver.

I find a death notice from a funeral
home saying her mother died a year ago
at the age of 91. I call the phone number
the search engine lists and get a recording:
The number you have reached is no longer in service.

In my black smock swimming with symbols
of goldfish that I bought in the boutique
in Hot Springs on the way to Pasadena
for one of her plays, I study the collage
in the hallway where Sandy and I stand
in our jeans, sweaters and flowered skirts,
she in her red hair flowing down her back
or in a ponytail and me in golden blonde
hair, permed sometimes, straight sometimes,
smiling like movie stars on the red carpet.

Martha Stewart Poses in Only an Apron at Age 81

I read the headlines on my 81ˢᵗ birthday
body covered from neck to ankles.
To cheer me up, my husband emails me
photos of me at sixty-five frolicking
on the beach in bikinis when I was a size six.
But I feel worse as I picture those bikinis
being worn by teenagers who shop at Goodwill.

I check out Martha's nudie photo. Big letdown.
I expect to see the Queen of the Kitchen
and Insider Trading Jailbird pouting
and posing like Marilyn Monroe had she lived
to be 81 in an apron wrapped around her waist
baring breasts, belly and legs, not a stranger

with salon styled and dyed blonde hair,
thin arms sticking out of an apron tied
around her neck looking bored and lifeless
as a mannequin at Macy's and holding
a coffee cup and cut off at her whittled
waist by a display of Pumpkin Spice Coffee.

I want this woman's skin smooth as syrup
so I click on the site that says: *Martha
Stewart shares a Vitamin C serum
that keeps her skin selfie ready.* There
she is smiling and she is the Martha

Stewart I remember. Botoxed, face lifted
and air brushed. Clearly not the face
of an octogenarian. I don't order the serum
but smear my face with dollar store anti
wrinkle cream and hope for the best.

EPILOGUE

The Leading Ladies in My Life

Death is just the last scene in the final act.
Joyce Carole Oates, *Blonde*

teach me to carefully
choose the roles
I audition for,
check out my co-star
before taking the part,
memorize my lines
before I speak, improvise
and not always
follow the script,
choose my wardrobe
wisely to blend in
like a chameleon
or bloom like a lily
in a spring rain,
know when to take
a bow and when
to exit the stage,
and most of all
to graciously accept
applause and praise
and critical reviews
and to die with dignity.

Last Woman Standing

One by one, the matriarchs
have disappeared from
the landscape of my life.
Grandmothers, mother,
aunts, female cousins.
Leaving me the oldest
surviving female
to tend the graves and guide
the younger generations.
Even though I am a grandmother
and great grandmother,
I feel ill prepared to walk
in the footsteps of these
strong women, carrying
the torch until I disappear
and a new matriarch
takes up the march.

ABOUT THE AUTHOR

Sharon Waller Knutson is a retired journalist who was born in Montana and now lives in Arizona. She has published ten poetry books including *My Grandmother Smokes Chesterfields (Flutter Press 2014,) What the Clairvoyant Doesn't Say* and *Trials & Tribulations of Sports Bob (Kelsay Books 2021) and Survivors, Saints and Sinners* and *Kiddos & Mamas Do the Darndest Things (Cyberwit 2022) and The Vultures are Circling (Cyberwit 2023.)* Her work has also appeared in more than 50 journals.